MEET
BLAKE
GRIFFIN

Basketball's Slam Dunk King

Ethan Edwards

PowerKiDS
press

New York

Published in 2014 by The Rosen Publishing Group, Inc.
29 East 21st Street, New York, NY 10010

First Edition

Editors: Joshua Shadowens and Jennifer Way
Book Design: Greg Tucker
Book Layout: Kate Vlachos
Photo Research: Katie Stryker

Photo Credits: Cover; pp. 4, 8, 18, 30 © (2013, 2011, 2013) Getty Images. Photos by Stephen Dunn/ Getty Images; p. 7 © (2010, 2013) Getty Images. Photo by Jeff Gross/Getty Images; p. 9 Ned Dishman/ Contributor/Getty Images Sport/Getty Images; p. 11 Peter G. Aiken/Contributor/Getty Images Sport/ Getty Images; p. 12 Jamie Squire/Staff/Getty Images Sport/Getty Images; p. 14 © (2009) Getty Images. Photo by Jim McIsaac/Getty Images; pp. 15, 19, 20 © (2010, 2011, 2011) Getty Images. Photo by John W. McDonough/Getty Images; p. 17 © (2011) Getty Images. Photo by Harry How/Getty Images; p. 23 © (2013) Getty Images. Photo by Pool/Getty Images; p. 24 © (2012) Getty Images. Photo by Mark Ralston/ Getty Images; pp. 25, 29 © (2013, 2013) Getty Images. Photo by Frederic J. Brown/Getty Images; p. 26 John Sciulli/Staff/Getty Images Sport/Getty Images.

Library of Congress Cataloging-in-Publication Data

Edwards, Ethan.
  Meet Blake Griffin : basketball's slam dunk king / by Ethan Edwards. — First edition.
    pages cm — (All-star players)
  Includes index.
  ISBN 978-1-4777-2913-7 (library binding) — ISBN 978-1-4777-3002-7 (pbk.) —
ISBN 978-1-4777-3073-7 (6-pack)
  1. Griffin, Blake, 1989-—Juvenile literature. 2. Basketball players—United States—Biography—Juvenile
literature. I. Title.
  GV884.G76E38 2014
  796.323092—dc23
  [B]
                              2013019881
Manufactured in the United States of America

CPSIA Compliance Information: Batch #W14PK2: For Further Information contact Rosen Publishing, New York, New York at 1-800-237-9932

Contents

Here is Griffin during a 2013 NBA play-off game against the Memphis Grizzlies.

Slam Dunks

Many basketball fans love the game because **slam dunks** are so exciting to watch. No one dunks better than Blake Griffin. Griffin is the star **power forward** of the Los Angeles Clippers. A power forward's job is to get down the court near the basket for scoring and for **rebounding**. It helps if a power forward is tall. Griffin stands at 6 feet 10 inches (2.08 m) tall. That is almost 7 feet (2.13 m) tall!

Some fans and basketball writers think he is the best power forward in the game. He is also a great leader who has helped transform the struggling Clippers team into a winner.

All-Star Facts

Griffin is known for his sense of humor and for being a funny guy. He would love to host the TV show *Saturday Night Live* someday.

Blake Griffin was born on March 16, 1989, in Oklahoma City, Oklahoma. His family loved sports. Blake's father owned a store that made trophies. He also coached high-school basketball. Blake and his older brother, Taylor, were both gifted youth athletes. Their mother homeschooled them both until they reached high school. Even though they were not in school, the Griffin brothers had no problems making friends and competing with other young athletes.

Blake became close friends with another young athlete named Sam Bradford. His family owned a gym. Blake and Sam spent hours playing basketball there. Sam Bradford eventually went on to become a **professional** football player for the St. Louis Rams.

Griffin made this slam dunk in a 2010 game against the Minnesota Timberwolves. A slam dunk is worth two points in a basketball game.

Here Griffin keeps control of the ball while Marc Gasol of the Memphis Grizzlies tries to defend against him.

The father of the Griffin brothers coached at Oklahoma Christian School. It made perfect sense for Blake and Taylor to attend the school so they could play for his team. Together, they led the Oklahoma Christian School Saints to two state **championships**.

Taylor graduated and went on to college, and Blake led his high school to two more state championships. The Saints lost only six games during Blake's four years on the team. He was the most famous high-school basketball player in the whole state. The nation's top college coaches were watching him closely.

The Jordan Brand Classic is an all-star game for the best high-school basketball players in the United States. Blake Griffin (left) played in the 2007 game.

Sooner

The top college scouts decided that Blake Griffin was among the 20 best **recruits** from the whole country. Jeff Capel, the head coach at the University of Oklahoma, already knew what Blake could do. The Griffin family did not live far from the university, and Taylor already played for Capel. Blake decided to play basketball for the Oklahoma Sooners.

Griffin enjoyed an excellent freshman year, but he **injured** both knees. He was able to play, but his knee injuries would present challenges for years to come. Even with the knee injuries, Griffin was one of the top scorers in college basketball. Scouts from the National Basketball Association, or NBA, believed that Griffin was ready to leave college and play at the highest level of the game. Griffin, though, decided to return to Oklahoma and play another season for the Sooners.

Here is Griffin playing for the Oklahoma Sooners in a 2009 game against the Kansas State Wildcats.

Griffin played even better during his sophomore season. He recorded 30 **double-doubles** that year, including 40 points and 23 rebounds against Texas Tech. He also snagged 504 rebounds for the season. No college player had done this since the great Larry Bird in 1979! After two amazing years, Griffin was ready to become a professional basketball player.

All-Star Facts

Griffin loves practicing yoga. It is one of his favorite exercises.

One of Griffin's knee injuries happened during this 2008 game against the Kansas Jayhawks.

Welcome to Los Angeles

The Los Angeles Clippers had the first pick in the 2009 NBA **Draft**. The NBA draft takes place every year. It is a **lottery** system that allows the teams with the biggest needs to draft the best players. No team had bigger needs than the Los Angeles Clippers, and no one was surprised when they picked the best power forward in the draft.

Here NBA commissioner David Stern poses with Griffin after he was chosen to play for the Clippers.

Griffin (left) is sitting on the sidelines with his Clippers teammates before a game.

Clippers fans had been patient for a long time. There are two NBA teams in Los Angeles, the Lakers and the Clippers. The Lakers are one of the greatest NBA teams of all time. In the history of the NBA, only the Boston Celtics have been more successful and won more championships than the Lakers. The Clippers, however, are often called L.A.'s other team. They have yet to win a championship.

Clippers fans were excited about their new slam-dunking power forward. Surely Griffin could lead the team to greatness. Unfortunately, in the final **preseason** game in the summer of 2009, Griffin fractured his left kneecap when he landed wrong after a dunk. He needed to have **surgery** and would have to sit out the season. Clippers fans were disappointed. They would have to wait at least a year to see their new star in action.

Chris Bosh of the Miami Heat (left) is trying to keep Griffin from making a shot during a 2011 game.

Flying High

Griffin finally got to join the Clippers for the 2010–2011 regular season. He was ready, but his new team was not. Griffin played like a superstar, but basketball is a team sport.

This game against the Chicago Bulls took place during Griffin's first season playing with the Clippers.

Here is Griffin making one of his famous slam dunks in a game against the Chicago Bulls.

One great player cannot win games by himself. The team struggled, but Griffin just got better and better. He scored 44 points in a game against the New York Knicks. He scored 47 against the Indiana Pacers.

This photograph shows the Slam Dunk Contest during which Griffin leaped over a car to make his shot!

Griffin began to be known for his dunks. He seemed to fly through the air. He even dunked by jumping over other basketball stars. Clips began to appear all over the Internet showing some of his best dunks. He was named **Rookie** of the Year, and he became just the twentieth rookie in NBA history to average at least 20 points and 10 rebounds per game. Griffin was also picked to play in the All-Star Game. Each year, fans vote for the best players who they want to see face off in the All-Star Game. Since he was a rookie, Griffin was not the starting power forward for the Western Conference's team. He played well during his first All-Star Game, but he especially shined at the Slam Dunk Contest.

Each year, the All-Star Weekend events include a Slam Dunk Contest. Griffin did not let his fans down at the contest. He leaped over a Kia, a small car, that was parked on the basketball court. Griffin was the star he always knew he could be. Now it was time for the Clippers to catch up to him.

Before the 2011–2012 season, the Clippers decided to build a team around their young power forward. They brought Chris Paul, one of basketball's best **point guards**, to the team. A point guard leads the team by passing to the right player at the right time. A good point guard can get the ball to a power forward. Paul and Griffin immediately played well together, and the Clippers improved. Griffin made the All-Star team again, this time as a starter. He scored 22 points and helped the Western Conference win the game.

Griffin made this dunk during the 2013 All-Star Game. Because the Los Angeles Clippers are in the Western Conference, Griffin played for the Western Conference All-Star team.

Griffin is showing his stuff here while warming up for a game against the Heat that was played in China. The NBA hosts games in that country since the sport is growing in popularity there.

The Clippers finished the regular season with 40 wins. That was good enough to make the **play-offs**. Los Angeles faced the Memphis Grizzlies in the first round and beat them in a close series. Unfortunately, the Clippers were no match for the San Antonio Spurs in the next round.

Griffin was chosen to represent the United States in the 2012 Olympic Games in London, but he decided to stay behind. He had injured his left knee again and did not want to risk making it worse by playing in the Olympics. He wanted to take the time he needed to heal so that he would be in good shape for the Clippers' next season.

Griffin averaged 18 points per game in the 2012–2013 season. Here he's about to make a basket in a 2013 game against the Memphis Grizzlies.

Winning It All

Griffin and the Clippers returned to the play-offs at the end of the 2012–2013 season. This time they lost the first round against the Memphis Grizzlies. The Clippers fell short of winning a championship once again, but fans now hope that Griffin can help win one for them some day. The Clippers are no longer "L.A.'s other team." Griffin helps lead them to the play-offs year after year.

The superstar power forward helped turn the Clippers around in a very short time. They are one of the NBA's best teams, and most fans would agree that Griffin is the NBA's most exciting slam dunker.

Griffin's slam-dunking ability has helped the Los Angeles Clippers earn more fans.

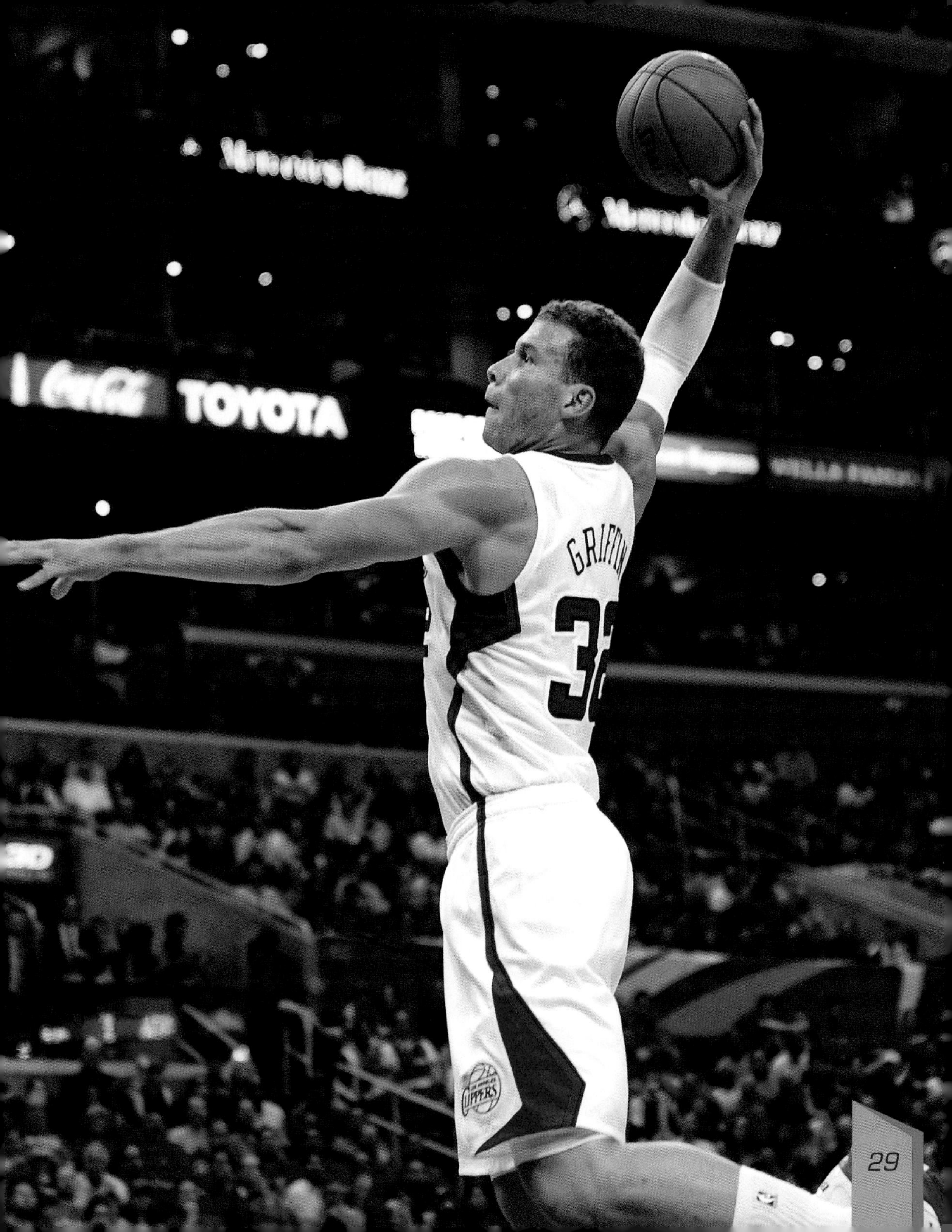
TOYOTA
GRIFFIN
32

Stat Sheet

Team: Los Angeles Clippers
Position: Power Forward
Uniform Number: 32
Born: March 16, 1989
Height: 6 feet 10 inches
        (2.08 m)
Weight: 250 pounds (113 kg)

Season	Team	Points per game	Rebounds per game	Assists per game	Free-Throw Percentage
2010–2011	Clippers	22.5	12.1	3.8	.642
2011–2012	Clippers	20.7	10.9	3.2	.521
2012–2013	Clippers	18.0	8.3	3.7	.660

Glossary

championships (CHAM-pee-un-ships) Contests held to determine the best, or the winner.

charity (CHER-uh-tee) A group that gives help to the needy.

double-doubles (DUH-bul-DUH-bulz) Basketball games in which a player gets double-digit numbers in two of five categories.

draft (DRAFT) The selection of people for a special purpose.

injured (IN-jurd) Harmed or hurt.

lottery (LAH-tuh-ree) The drawing of lots used to decide something. Lots are objects used as counters in a lottery.

obesity (oh-BEE-suh-tee) The condition of being very overweight.

play-offs (PLAY-ofs) Games played after the regular season ends to see who will play in the championship game.

point guards (POYNT GAHRDZ) Basketball players who direct their teams' forward plays on the court.

power forward (POW-er FOR-werd) A basketball player who gets the ball into position for scoring. Power forwards also make many rebounds.

preseason (PREE-see-zun) A time right before the start of the regular season when players train.

professional (pruh-FESH-nul) Someone who is paid for what he or she does.

rebounding (REE-bownd-ing) Getting control of the ball after a missed shot.

recruits (rih-KROOTS) New members of groups.

rookie (RU-kee) A new major-league player.

scouts (SKOWTS) People who help sports teams find new, young players.

slam dunks (SLAM DUNKS) Basketball shots made by jumping high enough to throw the ball down into the basket.

surgery (SER-juh-ree) An operation.

Index

Websites

Due to the changing nature of Internet links, PowerKids Press has developed an online list of websites related to the subject of this book. This site is updated regularly. Please use this link to access the list: www.powerkidslinks.com/asp/griffi/